The Cinematic Cat

A Cat's Guide to the Great Movies

The Cinematic Cat

A Cat's Guide to the Great Movies

CREATED, WRITTEN AND PRODUCED
BY BOB BRUNO

ILLUSTRATED BY MARGUERITE CHADWICK

A & W Visual Library
New York

An A & W Visual Library book
Published by
A & W Publishers, Inc.
95 Madison Avenue
New York, New York 10016

Manufactured in the United States of America
Designed by Denise Schiff
1   2   3   4   5   6   7   8   9   10

Library of Congress Cataloging in Publication Data

Bruno, Bob.
   The cinematic cat.

   1. Moving-pictures—Anecdotes, facetiae, satire, etc.
2. Cats—Anecdotes, facetiae, satire, etc.   I. Chadwick, Marguerite.   II. Title.
PN6231.M7B7   791.43′75′0207   81-70449
                                         AACR2

ISBN 0-89104-289-X

Acknowledgments

If it wasn't for our cat-loving agent, Pat Loud, and her associate, Bobbi Munro, this book would have remained an idea. We owe a lot to them.

Loving thanks to Peter, who really put up with a lot.

Special thanks to Fred, Keith, Mike, Randi, Steve, and Tom.

And, of course, thanks to Ernest and Julio, our inspirations.

*Bue and
Marguerite*

Tucked away in the hills of Hollywood is the Tom and Jerry Residence for Retired Performing Felines where, under the shade of lush catnip trees, resides an assortment of the most famous show biz cats in the world. This is where they come to rest—far from the madding crowd—to live out their sunset years in the style to which they have become accustomed. The buzz of the cattail party set has it that even the fabulous recluse Greta Purrbo is living within the dog-resistent walls of TJ's. But of course, no one can be absolutely positive since these famous faces are always hidden behind the TJ-issue-no-peek sunglasses.

Muscular young attendants (who are all waiting for their big break) scamper along and perform a variety of tasks. Catering to the needs of the residents is their primary concern. With utmost dedication they prepare sumptuous gourmet meals to suit the whims and whiskers of their illustrious charges. And at a steady pace, the handsome young actors push wheelchairs, fluff pillows, and tuck in blankets as they wheel the likes of Truman Catpote and Lauren BaCat down the pool.

The mood is set to a moderate tempo, with the piped-in purring of a PA system—soothing to the minds of the great. Most conversations take place in the past tense—with continual reminiscences and references to the best clips of their lives.

The pretty actresses who work at TJ's conduct daily tummy-tightening classes for all those playcats of yesteryear. Burt, Warren, Jack and the legendary Rudolph Valenkitty eagerly attend these lessons every morning. The girls swoon at Warren's smiles, melt when Burt does a set of push-ups and long to have their tails ruffled by Jack or Rudie.

By the time Julio arrived at TJ's he had directed and produced scores of Hollywood's most memorable films. He was truly a cat among cats, and although now in his mature years he is still charismatic and dapper. Even in his youth his whiskers were snow white so that one of the betraying signs of age has never shown on him. His coat is black and sleek and his face an ermine white mask—with a touch of jet black on his chin.

From noon 'til three every afternoon you can find Julio lounging under the tallest catnip tree dictating his thoughts and fond memories about the celebrities and films that have spanned his career....

The Sound of Music, 1965

Julie Angora sheds the cloth for the fur and with her Osmondesque troupe of seven sings up and down the Austrian Alps. They successfully slip by the paws of the Nazis to the tune of fun meows and the music of Tenders and Vittlestein. Available on videodisc: good investment.

West Side Story, 1961

Catalie Would becomes a minority, takes singing lessons and disturbs the ghetto balance of nature. Lots of flying fur, fence climbing and moonlight. It's Shakespeare, but Bernstein, Sondheim and Robbins make it surreal. Singing in line outside the theater is a must. [Wear your Cons.]

Gypsy, 1962

Catalie Would joins a different kind of minority and forgets how to sing. If Rosalind Rusttail only had the money she had in *Mame,* they could have started at the Kitkat Klub. Karl Molten, without his American Express card, is terrific but poor. Revealing score. Cute kittens in modest dress.

The King and I, 1956

Another Tenders and Vittlestein hit. The King of Siam (Yummies Brynner) hires a British schoolteacher (Tabbie Kerr) to tutor his royal litter. The king goes bald, and Brynner stars in the revival of '60, '64, '68, '72, '76, '80, et cetera, et cetera.

Cabaret, 1972

Between reichs, Liza Gatonelli does a few obscene moves on a chair, and Joel Spay talks about everyone in the neighborhood. A musical reminder that there's more to the Teutonic mind than Wagner. Pre–Berlin Wall and Volkswagen.

Bye-Bye Birdie, 1963

Pelvic twitches and *ennui* invade Smalltown, USA, when teen idol Catrad Birdie arrives. Ann-Margarine, typical Anykitten, is selected to bestow, on nationwide TV, America's last kiss on Birdie before he is inducted into the armed forces. Perfect elevator music. May cause diabetes.

Mary Poppins, 1964

Julie Angora, nanny *extraordinaire,* feeds
spoonfuls of sugar to Glynnis Tom's children, producing sidewalk hallucinations.
Dick Van Mitten has the chimney-sweep
concession, and blue-haired shopping-
bag lady gets prime seat for the Royal
Wedding.

Mame, 1974

Lucille Furball contributes to the delinquency of a minor after her hus-
band drops out of the picture. Fortunately, Beauregard owned a piece of
the Rock before falling from one, assuring enough loot to keep her in
caviar and caftans.

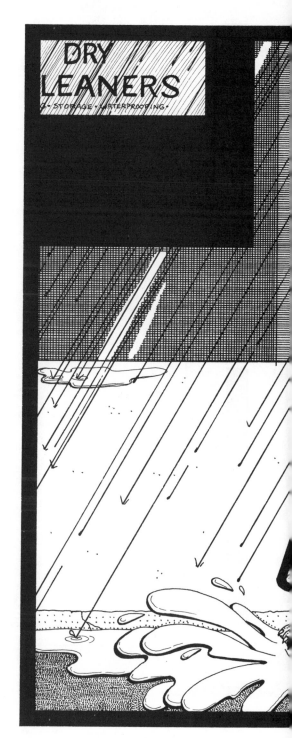

Singin' in the Rain, 1952

This film has only one scene, and it's done to music.
Preen Kelly is still doing it in Vegas and Atlantic City.

My Fair Lady, 1964

Rex Hairyson transforms a street cat into a royal kitten. Clawdrey Hepburn gets her tail coiffed and, after months of meowcution lessons, fools the court. Professor Mittens and Eliza Doolitter fall hopelessly in love, of course. Free with any purchase of the OED.

Funny Girl, 1968

Barbara Straysand as Fanny Mice is perfect. Whatever she tries brings on a round of ap-paws. Omar Sharpteeth lives up to his name, and Fanny turns tails up to him. Cats who need cats are the luckiest cats.

King Creole, Kid Galahad, Jailhouse Rock, Viva Las Vegas, GI Blues and Clambake, 1950s/1960s

Elvis Prowley wears a guitar, catches a girl, loses a girl, has a fight, wins a girl, sings a song on a ranch, in the Army, in jail, on the beach, in a nightclub, in Vegas and in the ring. Just change his costume.

Frankenstein, 1932

Borrowed paws, whiskers and tail are the basic ingredients you need for this at-home-instruction film that demonstrates how to build your own monster cat. The finished product, which has a striking resemblance to Boris Katoff, is a guaranteed neighborhood dog-stopper. Paper towels may be used instead of gauze to help offset an exorbitant electric bill.

Bride of Frankenstein, 1935

Boris Katoff, on the third of nine lives, is presented with Elsa Lancheshire, who is only on her second. In this forerunner of *The Dating Game,* the two 'Steins, worried about inbreeding from the same mold, don't exactly see scar to scar, and the whole affair ends in a mess. Great coif and hiss.

Young Frankenstein, 1974

Mel Boots's interpretation of the classic story. Madeline Kaht successfully gives us another use for a dead cat. Cats under seventeen should not be admitted.

The Birds, 1963

Tippi Excedrin's headache number 1,233 intensifies after exposure to Suzanne Plushette's acting and Rod Tailer's investing in down comforters. Summer tourist trade slips to all-time low in small coastal village. Available on special let's-stay-home-this-holiday cassette with *Jaws* on the reverse side.

Psycho, 1960

Alfred Pitchblack's unforgettable thriller starring pretty Janet Flea and weird Tony Purrkins. One step beyond *Oedipus Rex.* This film introduces a clever strategy for eliminating houseguests. Originally filmed in black and white, the laserdisk version comes with a complete set of Venus Paradise coloring pencils.

Jaws, 1975

Man-eating catfish goes to the Cape for the summer but would rather be in Martha's Vineyard—alone. His need for solitude eats away at the tourists until they all decide to leave. Suddenly he has every beach in America to himself for the mid-1970s. The Kennedys enjoy the peace and quiet. Available in a special edition with *The Birds*.

What Ever Happened to Baby Jane, 1962

Puss Davis and Joan Clawford get to demonstrate their true feelings for each other. Filled with good clawing. They go right for the jugular. Canary crudité. Parental discretion advised.

The Exorcist, 1973

Linda Hair manages to scare the living daylights out of her mom, the neighbors and the audience with her devilish antics. You'll want to wring her neck, but she does it first. Bring your rosary beads.

The Wizard of Oz, 1939

Judy Petland and Toto blow the Kansas scene and encounter a bizarre assortment of characters, the kind you would expect to meet at Studio 54. Small, scared dog and big, courageous cat have important roles. Must be seen at least once a year.

Miracle on 34th Street, 1947

Macy's invents the Christmas rush but claims, to the chagrin of little girls around New York who want to move to the suburbs on Long Island, that there is no Santa Claws. The day is saved, however, by the US Post Office's monumental decision to de-zip the North Pole. Great fun for the entire family: see it during the Thanksgiving weekend every year, then go out and shop.

Bringing Up Baby, 1938

Catrine Hepburn has some fun with a very large cat to
the dismay of Cary Pant. This is not a musical, but one
certain catchy tune turns Baby into a pussycat.

The African Queen, 1952

Catrine Hepburn and Humphrey Bocat wish for insect repellent halfway down some African river in a love boat. Bocie winds up in the lower berth more times than he'd like. The Germans are a nuisance.

Gone With the Wind, 1939

The all-time classic that finally explains the invention of polyester. As the cotton burns, Clark Kibble learns to live with just the shirt on his back and Vivian Flea declares that everyday is Thursday, to the delight of the help. People escape the Atlanta heat via a graffiti-less underground railroad.

Gone With the Wind

The Gay Divorcée, 1934

Fred Astray, using a few new tricks, taps himself into the heart of Ginger Livers. As usual, the steps are more complicated than the plot, but who cares. Controversial title.

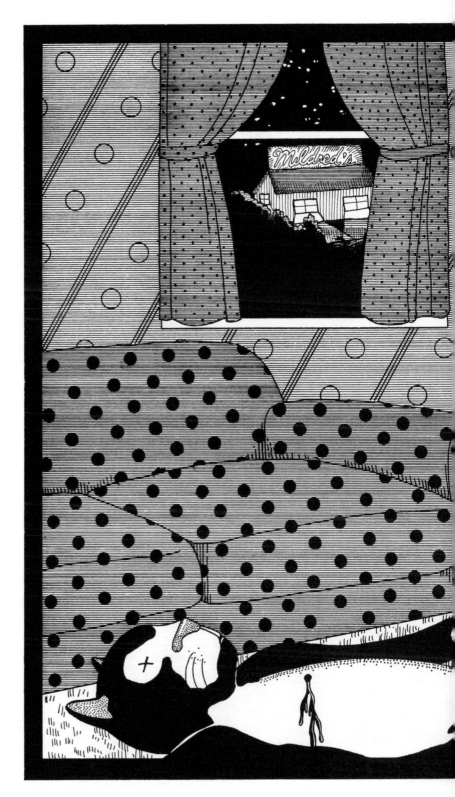

Mildred Pierce, 1945

Joan Clawford packs them in, shoulder to shoulder, with her renowned cuisine and free lessons in child rearing. Ann Blight apparently doesn't like the food and starts her own school of hubbycide, while Mom tries for the Girl Scout Merit Badge for Lying. Ms. Clawford gives good eyebrow.

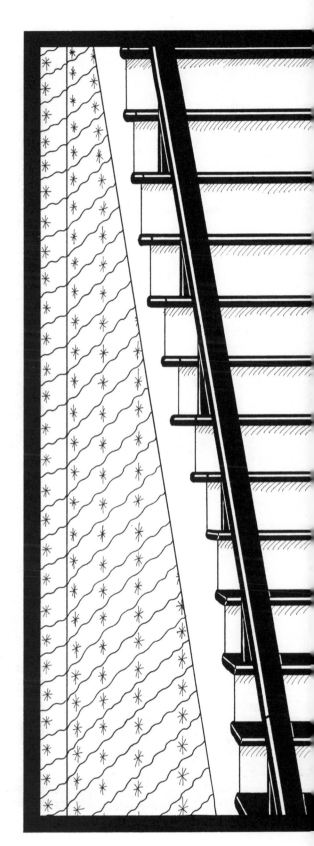

The Littlest Rebel, 1935

Shirley Tidbit shares a McIntosh with Lincoln after she and the help do a tap rendition of *Gone with the Wind*. Cute curls and diplomacy.

Sunset Boulevard, 1950

Some cats just don't take to water in this magnificent classic. Starring the one and only Clawdria Swansong as Nova Despot, a kitty of the Silent Screen who thinks she can meow them to death in the talkies. Get ready for the close-up.

Around the World in Eighty Days, 1958

Manx Niven thinks he can do it in a balloon. The making of the movie was plagued by as many problems as the NASA space program, but it costs a few billion dollars less to see than to film. Colorful and funny, he visits the Abyssinians, Burmese, Himalayans, Persians and Siamese. Just like a Club Med tour.

King Kong, 1933

Fur Wray has a thing for the hirsute and hits the jackpot in this million-dollar-movie classic. Finding an apartment with a view can be hard, no matter who you are. The first of many subway derailments.

Arthur, 1981

Liza Gatonelli is shoplifting in the best store in town when she meets Dudley Morris, her ticket to riches, a Rolls and a lifetime supply of Bon Vivant cat food. A painful wedding but terribly proper valet. And Lionels.

Annie Hall, 1977

Woody Alley, a nice Jewish cat from Brooklyn, emerges from therapy after fifteen years. Diane Kitten opens the Annie Hall Shop on One at Bloomingdale's. Woody suffers from chronic therapy withdrawal. Deductible on GHI and major medical.

It's a Mad, Mad, Mad, Mad World, 1963

Probably the longest cross-country treasure hunt and cat-and-mouse chase on celluloid. Like the number of *mad*s in the title, this film has too many stars to list here, certainly enough to keep Rona Furret talking for a week. The loot is buried under a *W,* but no one seems to know what that means.

The Seven Year Itch, 1955

When the wife-cat's away, Tom Stool goes scratching at Meowlyn Monroe's door, but Meowlyn manages to keep tick spray around, which helps her flee to her next modeling assignment on time. Purring.

The Odd Couple, 1968

Felix Lemmon and Whiskers Matthau play two not-so-typical ex-marrieds who have not-so-typical salaries and not-so-typical jobs and find a not-so-typical large apartment in a not-so-typically fashionable part of Manhattan and yet are confronted with the typical roommate problem—one's a slob and the other's a compulsive. Would have made a great article for *Apartment Life.* Why not switch to *Metropolitan Home,* and live alone?

The Road to Zanzibar, 1941

Between Singapore and Morocco, the Hollywood travellettes—Bing Crossbreed, Dorothy Lapawr and Altered Hope—pick up the beat in swinging Zanzibar, where they get themselves into more trouble. Take away their Getaway card and bring the boys home.

Cleopatra, 1963

Elizabeth Tailor does the legwork for the upcoming King Tut exhibit but barges in on the Roman Empire just as they are perfecting the art of assassination. Richard Purrton has his moment at the top of the pyramid. Clawdette Colbert is overthrown.

Bonnie and Clyde, 1967

Warren Breedy, Faye Furaway and Meowchal J. Pollard are major share-holders in a company that reinvests other people's money and does light human exterminating. Rated *G* by the National Rifle Association.

Doctor Zhivago, 1965

During the longest winter on record, the Commie pinkos confiscate Julie Friskie's caviar and don't give Omar Sharpteeth a chance to defrost his moustache. Borschtlike battle scenes. Not reviewed by Tass.

The Godfather, 1972

Producer bets on the wrong horse and tries not to lose his head over it. Highway tolls *can* be murder. Al Purrcino marries an island girl during a Ragu commercial, and then inherits the family business after Marlon Catdo swallows too many marbles.

The Agony and the Ecstasy, 1969

Rex Hairyson pontificates on his Roman digs as Charlton Hisston, his interior decorator, spends time worrying about patterns. Creative ideas for fixing up your studio. Italian provincial.

The Ten Commandments, 1956

Based on the best-seller that depicts how the Egyptian dogs mistreated the Israelcats many years BC. The leading role of Morris is portrayed by that old whiskered tabby, Charlton Hisston. Yummies Brynner shines as the pharaoh. Tricky cure for aquaphobia.

The Graduate, 1967

Dustand Fleaman skillfully keeps his tail between his legs as he does it with an older woman, learns the real meaning of plastic, and rides around southern California in a bus with some pretty kitty in a white dress. Morris Nichols got a cash advance from MasterCard to produce this film—it's worth the 18 percent interest.

Guess Who's Coming to Dinner, 1967

What to do about crossbreeding and what the neighbors will think are the central themes of this film. Catrine Hepburn and Sylvester Tracy don't want to be the first on the block with a mixed grandlitter—leave it to the Joneses. Pretty house and garden. See it with a liberal.

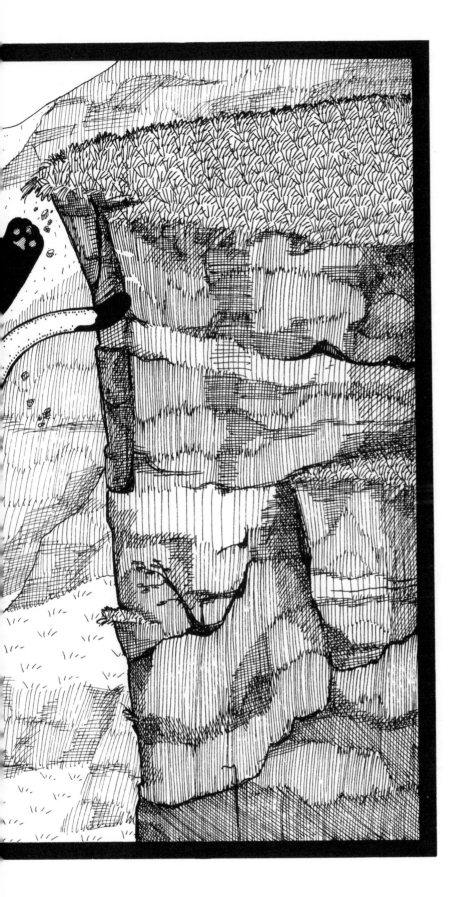

Butch Cassidy and the Sundance Kid, 1969

Dropping out of sight is easy for Paul Newcat and Robert Redpoint after a long day working the railroad. Katherine Fluff rides on a handlebar. Would have had a happy ending if their travel agent had suggested a cruise.

The Lion in Winter, 1968

Rome says no. A marriage counselor recommends separate castles for Peter O'Tail and Catrine Hepburn, who sharpens her claws between holidays. Quite catty. No one worries about what the children think, because they can't.

True Grit, 1969

Clawn Wayne gives us the quintessential Western in which the bad guys
make the good guys angry, so they go after the bad guys who shoot at the
good guys who shoot at the bad guys and eliminate a few good guys who
eventually defeat the bad guys. All this is done without any help from
Glenn Collarbell.

A Streetcar Named Desire, 1951

Blanche du Chat's tail grows with each tale she tells, but all unfolds when Stanley Catawalski changes his T-shirt. Marlon Catdo doesn't miss a flex. See it if you're in a good mood and don't want to be.

R's & X's

Tom Jones, 1963

Buxom female eats oysters, and Albert Finicky invents the art of sensuous dining. It's eighteenth-century England—do you know who your mother is? Lots of procreation.

10, 1979

Dudley Morris goes head-over-paws for Bo Purrfect's interpretation of *Bolero*. Long, rhythmic crescendo. Definitely for the decimal-minded.

Midnight Cowboy, 1969

Country cat Tiger Voight has to do more than whistle for his 9-Lives during his short prowl in New York City. Dustand Fleaman knows every alley in town. Together they give up on the Apple and move to that New York suburb—Florida.

Superman, 1978

Ween Hackman surrounds himself in Grand Central Modern furnishings, while Margot Litter portrays the typical reporter struggling to make ends meet in a penthouse garden apartment. Christofur Reeve commutes in style. Posh igloo.

Star Wars, 1977

The sky's the limit as the real estate market takes off with the concept of stellar mobile homes. Catnap Fisher has a hard time collecting taxes, and Manx Hamill studies to become one with est. Far-out singles bar.

The Stepford Wives, 1975

Katherine Fluff notices that she is the only housecat in surburban Connecticut that doesn't purr while doing housework. Close to unraveling the mystery of her neighbors' domestic bliss, she gets her tail caught in a converted microwave, which to this day causes her to purr the joys of laundry, cooking and cleaning.

Godzilla, 1956

Big thing with a yen for raw Japanese emerges from that interminable museum of natural history on the ocean floor. He or she pussyfoots around Tokyo, Kyoto and other anagrams, only to be felled by too much power. Take the kittens to the Saturday matinee—you should remain outside, or wait until it comes around to your Sony. Available on Beta I and II only.